D1598474

THE
MAKING
OF
COLLATERAL
BEAUTY

Mark Yakich

TUPELO PRESS

The Making of Collateral Beauty
Copyright © 2006 Mark Yakich
ISBN-13: 978-1-932195-22-4
ISBN 10: 1-932195-22-X
Printed in Canada
LCCN: 2005903063

Grateful acknowledgment is made to the following publications in
which some of these pieces first appeared in somewhat different
form: *580 Split, Cue, Diagram,* and *River City*. A special thanks to
Fred Tomaselli and the James Cohan Gallery for permission
to use "Field Guides" on the cover.

This book is a work of the imagination. Any resemblance to
real persons or events is panegyrical.

First paperback edition January 2006

Tupelo Press
PO Box 539, Dorset, Vermont 05251
802.366.8185 • Fax 802.362.1883
editor@tupelopress.org • web www.tupelopress.org

Cover and text designed by William Kuch, WK Graphic Design

Cover painting: *Field Guides* by Fred Tomaselli,
James Cohan Gallery (jamescohan.com) used by permission.

Contents

A Note on the Notes

1   The Mountain

2   You Are Not a Statue

3   The Sunset

4   The Departure

5   Postcard to Ricardo and His Daughter Echo

6   Before Losing Yourself Completely to Love

7   Dreams Hardly Ever Seem to Change Things for the Better

9   Blazon

10   The Invisible Man's Daughter

11   Prose Sonnet

12   The Ordinary Sun

13   Blind Girl's Litany

14   Pastoral

15   Songs of Salience and Ambience

16   Index of Lawn Bowling or Index of Teenage Intimacy

17   Trireme

18   Character in the Real World

19   Stone Fruit

20   Saturday Night

21   Matinee

22   The Teller is the Only Survivor of the Fairy Tale Ending

23   Every Force Deserves a Form

24   Reluctant Prophet

25   Poem

26   Against Elegy

27   Good Mouth

28   Self-Portrait with Still Life

Shakespeare led a life of Allegory; his works are the comments on it.

—John Keats

A Note on the Notes

None of these notes is necessary in order to be entertained, instructed, or mauled by the apodictic poems in Mr. Yakich's book *Unrelated Individuals Forming a Group Waiting to Cross*. None of these notes is necessary, that is, unless you are a native speaker of German. Thought to be an ugly language in America, German is in reality as beautiful as French. The most beautiful word in German is actually Austrian: Zwetschkenknödel. It means *plum dumpling*. *Plum dumpling* would be the most beautiful word in English if it were not two words.

The Mountain

This poem begins with a line found under my sister's hat as it laid on a bench in the European wing of the Metropolitan Museum of Art. We weren't even looking at the Balthus painting "The Mountain" from which the poem derives its novel name. The poem was first called "Seven Ways of Dying a Little Girl's Hair," but I couldn't decide on a color. The knife-sharpening of the pencil halfway through the poem really happened. Every morning our father would take a kitchen knife and sharpen our pencils. He made it look so easy that one morning I decided I would try. That is how I lost a good chunk of flesh from the knuckle of my left index finger. It didn't hurt until I saw the blood. That's when I fainted. When I came to, my sister was fanning me with one of our grandfather's dirty handkerchiefs. Our grandfather lived with us until I was 12. He lived in the den because he had no legs with which to climb the stairs; they had been shot off in so-called Big One. The walls of the den were lined with books, so that every time I went in to see him I felt as if he were the smartest man on earth. The books, my mother's and father's, were all nonfiction.

You Are Not a Statue

Life began as a translation from the Danish original. I wrote the original not knowing Danish myself, but only a Danish woman named Eva Green. She was a friend of my friend "the Viking" who threw dependable, starched-shirt dinner parties in Copenhagen. Eva and I met over the cod chowder. I proceeded to discuss the finer points of New England clam chowder and how best to get me drunk. The shirttail in the poem is real. But I have no idea how it got tied into a "diamond knot"—if anyone could tell me what a diamond knot is I would be grateful. I assume it's a mistranslation from the original.

The Sunset

While hiking up a tall hill in Berkeley, California, with my French friend Severine, we decided to steal a couple of plums from a neighbor's tree. We couldn't agree on whether the red or the yellow plums would taste best. Finally I snapped off a couple of the yellow ones. Severine knocked my hand sending the plums down the hill. We watched them roll and roll down and down until they were out of sight. We joked that they rolled all the way into the Bay. Then she knocked me to the ground and made love to me like something she forgot on her to-do list. One month later we married so that she could get a green card. A month after that I discovered that she was already married to someone else in order to get a green card. I asked her about this on our honeymoon night while we were playing Monopoly. She had Boardwalk and Park Place and all the yellow and green properties too. I was pissed. I told her I couldn't be the boot anymore.

The Departure

Having nothing to do with my sister, I wrote this poem in one sitting. It was 138 lines long. After many revisions I trimmed it down to three words: "Dick had Grace." I lived with those under my pillow for a few weeks, then I tore them up and started again. The reference to the Invisible Man's Daughter is based on my experiences with her in third grade. Her name was Stephanie Gottschalk and I tried to hold her hand until fifth grade. In sixth grade, I'd almost forgotten about her and then I heard a first-bell rumor that she made out with Billy Hermes at the movies. When I asked her about this, jokingly, she picked me up by my collar and shoved me against the lockers. "Don't you ever tell anybody about it," she demanded. "I promise I won't tell a soul," I said. (Dear Stephanie, I am sorry I never kissed you when I had the chance.)

Postcard To Ricardo and His Daughter Echo

Ricardo and Echo are two of my favorite people in the world. When I
met Echo she was five years old and liked to dress me up in women's
clothing. After hosting a Saturday morning radio program, we used to
have fashion shows for her father and my co-host Andy. Andy got
dressed up in women's clothing too, but I stole the show having been
an apprentice to my Aunt Maggie who owns a bridal boutique in
Cedar Rapids, Iowa. People assume that Iowa is a either a place for the
country's finest cows or for the country's most brilliant writers. A lot of
people from the coasts think Iowa is either Idaho or Ohio. On which
side of the Mississippi River does Iowa lie? It's not a trick question.
Even most Iowans don't know that a lot of *Huck Finn* actually takes
place on the Iowa side of the Mississippi. Mark Twain is so funny that
way. He always talked about his characters in a quaint way: "I had this
girl, didn't know what to do with her—so I threw her down a well."
Did Twain, in fact, agree with Rousseau's premise that people are
innately good until they enter the social world and then they are
innately bad? It doesn't really matter. What should be learned from
Huck Finn is that you never want to set an adventure story on a one-
way course downriver—you'll have no way of getting your characters
back upstream without ruining the story's ending.

Before Losing Yourself Completely to Love

When I was a kid, my mother harped on me for my unmade bed. But I didn't see the sense in making the bed since I was coming back to it soon. Then I started to see the world for what it really was. Each morning I would pull the bedspread over the disheveled sheets and blankets, leaving a lumpy mess underneath. The bed looked like it was occupied with a family of rats and snakes. Mother knew what I was doing, but she didn't like rats and snakes anymore than I did.

Dreams Hardly Ever Seem to Change Things for the Better

I used to drive trucks cross-country for U-Haul. It was a lot of fun until I wrecked a 25-footer on the Massachusetts turnpike and was summarily fired. I didn't like my boss, Philip (one "l"), anyway. Then I worked for a seed catalogue place in Portland, Oregon. That was good for a while until I accidentally sent the *full* minutes of the Executive Committee meeting to all of the Trustees, revealing a distinct taste for embezzlement on someone's behalf of no one I can mention here. I did like my boss (I was dating her, of course) but she had to lay me off after most of our seeds burned up in a blaze in the main warehouse, which was the end of the beginning of our relationship. Three months later when I drove into Tracy, California, I knew I had found home. Managed to get a job helping a disabled man dress himself every morning, clean up the house, tend the yard. It was easy work and he told me the craziest stories about his time in the Pacific during WWII. I'll never forget the story about his hand getting hacked up in the automatic potato peeler because his hospital ship had been hit by Japanese zero. (He admitted later that he didn't actually still feed the patients the potatoes; then he admitted that the whole thing was made-up, but that he really had gotten a purple star and then he got it out to show me. I said, *You mean purple heart, don't you?* But he waved it off, saying, *Yeah sure, heart, star—they were tossing medals to us in our cots like they was taffy from a parade float.*) For almost a year it was a great job, until he had an hospice-commencing heart attack. The old man's son cut me a nice severance check and I decided I'd had enough of the U.S. for a while. I thought I'd go look up Kelly K., a girl I used to date as a 24-year-old but wanted to date as a teenager. I'd heard she was in Germany with one of the armed forces. This was in 1990. I got her address from her mother in Algonquin, Illinois, (where we grew up) and we started to exchange one, five, and then twenty-page letters. (Man could she write and in the tiniest, slanted print, not that big bubble, girl handwriting.) Kelly K. took to my plan quite well and I ended up visiting her in Baden-Baden. This poem is about how Kelly K. didn't mind supporting me for the first six months I was in Baden-Baden and then how she kicked me out for supporting me for the first six months in Baden-Baden. That's what led me to where I am now, on a train headed south to Trieste where I hope to find the ghost of Joyce and the origin of the color yellow.

Blazon

The body truly is an amazing machine for worshipping the hug. But the question nags: How do you package a hug so that your daughter or son can have one after lunch at school? The bedroom ceiling has no answers, the kitchen counter ditto, the front door could care less about a hug but doesn't. It's one of those words you can't use very seriously in common parlance. Embrace is much prettier, but not a lot of fun to use on a child.

The Invisible Man's Daughter

After the tree house incident, I asked her: If one could write out one's life faster than one could live it, would that constitute time travel? She just glared at me, "I suppose some people enjoy bad writing, but I am not one of them. Let me pass, you." I released my hold of the "breathing multiplicity of the text," as my old friend Scott William likes to call singing, and handed her the rope. I thought she was going to hang herself with it (her father having recently died), but instead she tied me up and tickled my forearms with z's.

Prose Sonnet

The shirt in the poem was real, the house was not, and the last line was stolen from a philosopher who was in love with a 13-year-old boy. The attic window from which the reader views all of this alleged failing in love was pentagonal, red and yellow stained glass. Over the years, many neighborhood kids have tried to knock out the window with rocks and baseballs, but it can only be smashed from the inside out.

The Ordinary Sun

New Yorkers assume that the pastoral scene depicted here takes place in Central Park. Chicagoans assume the location is Grant Park. Parisians believe it to be Jardin du Luxembourg. Of course this is only pointed out because one should appreciate the power of people's intuition. Nevertheless, the poem takes places in Gori, Georgia, in 1889. The boy in the poem, who has stolen his father's razor, is J.V. Stalin. And the "unknown end" is the imminent deaths of eight million intuitions by his verbal signature. The light at the end of the poem is symbolic of the kind of life one wishes to lead but can't because one has been born a human being, a Cossack, a daughter. The absence, therefore, that surrounds the poem makes the light work hard.

Blind Girl's Litany

Based on a girl I knew in elementary and high school. Her name was Dori and she died 12 years ago. She was 21. By contrast, Huck Finn was never alive but he will live forever. What memory is to matter, matters least. I haven't thought about Dori in three years—I record each time I do. "What the fuck do you care?" she used to say, "that I got Hodgkins." She said it like a punch line, and she never used the word disease. Or carcinogen. Or Rasputin. For a long time kids thought she meant an imaginary friend named Hotchkiss. But who still has an imaginary friend in high school? Before I wrote this poem, I talked to Dori. I tried to reassure her about being dead, that despite her protests, it's not so awful. See, I said, I haven't talked to my mother in 73 days, but it's not worth writing down.

Pastoral

The American Association of Pastoral Counselors refuses to sanction this poem, one way or the other. [It always is disappointing when a poet fails to move a reader in any-which-way; this is a tent I raise later in "Gentle Reader."] The Association's "Summary of Findings," however, does offer an interesting formation:

"...research found that an overwhelming number of Americans [sic] recognize the close link between spiritual faith, religious values, and economic holy lands, and would prefer to seek assistance from a mental health professional who can integrate spiritual values into the course of petroleum products..."

- 83 percent feel their spiritual faith and religious beliefs are closely tied to their state of mental and emotional health, if and only if they don't have to drop off the kids at school, commute to work in an automobile, or use hair coloring products.

- 77 percent of respondents say it is important to see a pastoral counselor who knows how to keep quiet during a pornographic movie.

- 72 percent say it would be important for an elderly parent who was in need of medical mental treatment to get assistance from a pastoral professional who knew how and when to bitch-slap a grown child for crying gratuitously.

- 64 percent believe many a fertilizer passes for perfume.

- 29 percent mention pastoral counselors, more often than any other professionals, in conjunction with the expression "permission-slip cruelty."

Songs of Salience and Ambience

Fact is, I never chase the whales. I anchor a boat, sometimes for weeks at a time, and only project from that location. If the whales are interested in what I offer, they'll swim to me. I never transmit louder than the volume of a ten horse-power outboard. Because my goal is direct communication between species, I never play recorded music to the whales. Nor do I rely on electronic effects that reflect the whales' own calls back at them. Although a whale can certainly answer the mood and tones of a recording, a recording cannot answer a whale. I am not willing, you see, to prosper according to victory, shipwrecks, or proportionate response.

Index of Lawn Bowling or Index of Teenage Intimacy

A memorandum on the movie version of this poem: it's bound to be bad. But I still hope it's made during my lifetime. The only place I know it will be made satisfactorily is if you and I were to sleep together. Not the actual moment of syncopation, but the reticulation that follows.

Trireme

According to Webster's (preferable to the petite bourgeoisism of the OED), trireme is "an ancient galley having three banks of oars." If you had to look it up like a good Nabokovian, feel proud (pride being as reprehensible as war), so did I. Often I mistake a trireme for a lateen on ancient ships. This has never been my problem in the bedroom, however; I check all metaphors, like wet umbrellas, at the door.

Character in the Real World

It's true. There were a great number of consequential lovers, especially after a certain Bulgarian-Pole (who knows who she is, though often denies who she is in favor of the Platonic ideal which, incidentally, has led to most of history's problems or what at least defines itself as history.) I, like Elia Kazan, only name names when they get in the way of making love.

Stone Fruit

It boils down to whether or not the girl really did lather her chest with honey and invite bees to sting her, hoping her breasts would remain engorged afterwards.

Saturday Night

Based on a Hal Hartley movie, yes. Based on an Amish love of Parker
Posey, yes. Based on a crime scene photo, no. Based on a real crime,
maybe. Based on two rats which I found fornicating in the crawl
space while I went looking for the escaped stray cat and which I was
planning on beating to death with a baseball bat, no. Based on the fact
that unspeakable actions are our epics: it's still too early to tell. The
rate of incarceration is phenomenal; the domination of sentences
likewise. In the movies nobody cries like Sean Penn.

Matinee

After debating whether Jews believe in any kind of afterlife with my friend Scott (who likes to call himself General P.T. Beauregarde), The General slashed off my head for using the f-word. I picked my head up and left. The evening sun was going down the sky's transom and I could see (out of my one good eye) that it was going to be a Guinness night. I didn't know what had come over The General, really. We had been good friends ever since he stayed with my parents and me as a middle school exchange student. He hadn't been so fat then and he preferred vegetables (especially corn on the cob) to my mother's meat dishes and anchovy casseroles. As I walked home I thought: Where do we, in fact, make post-college, post-Cold War friends? I decided that it was going to be with the childhood friend I had always hoped for and never got. Why, I thought, can one not re-return to one's past and make something new of it? Return even to someone else's past and do what one will. The Romans after all used Egyptian coffins in which to take their baths. When I got home, I found a boy balancing himself on the rail of my balcony. I said, "Quit fooling around up there!" And he turned to me and said, "It might feel like suicide if you blow on me from there. But if you come closer, I'll show you how to cry without tears."

The Teller is the Only Survivor of the Fairy Tale Ending

I wrote this poem to Chang Hsu after drinking. The hypothesis was: Must Western writers shun happiness? And if so, why so? See, you learn things by doing them the way you didn't start out thinking *Thy will be done.* Classical: Faulkner wanted to write poems, got novels; Shakespeare wanted to marry someone he loved, got plays; Yahweh wanted to create a small garden, got a compost patch. Each writer limits herself to the story of her own execution. Once upon a time when I was working in the dark age without a plague, a young man in a peaceable suit cut me to shreds for a budget. I felt practically ministerial. *Yes,* at last I wrote, *one forges one's own.* But vernacular soldiers never get home.

Every Force Deserves a Form

In our age italics are overused. Like celebrities. Humans created God because no one else was well-drawn. The old chain-gang trick. Our story got told from one point-of-view to another so many times that by the time the story reached the first person, the story had turned the squiggle and the writer into a pair of illicit lovers carelessly smoking a cigarette after sex and walking around the house naked in stitches. Then the squiggling pen really did begin to look pretty—so pretty that the writer-cum-blunderer decided to do something about it before anybody saw. Of course, somebody did see and soon the whole place was chasing a new beginning. Then someone created God. Oops! It was an aleatory act, a moment when the pen slipped a little causing the writer to forget about the number of eggs gathered from the hens, and that the weather was usually foggy in the morning but sunny by early afternoon. Beautiful and boring. Sweet and tedious: fucking San Francisco (the boy-saint, not the city-state). In the beginning, someone said something and then somebody else wrote it down. In the beginning, a man lived and was about to get hitched. A woman took down the flour from the shelf, started to make a cake. Unfortunately she was blamed when it tasted nothing like a wedding.

Reluctant Prophet

I knew a man who laughed to himself more than ever at the dinner table. He had been in remission from something I still don't know how to pronounce correctly, and I wondered if being in remission didn't have something to do with his laughing. His eyes were deep brown, very unlike pools or cat's eyes, and his eyelashes were too thin to see from across the table. And he didn't look ill. Once I asked him what was so funny. He seemed confused and a little embarrassed, and I never asked him again. Because I first met him a long time ago, I don't remember it very well. It was the beginning of a tepid, uneventful summer. He had just finished working on the guidance system for the Apollo that went to the moon. A few years later, he was the first person to show me how a plane is able to take off. I felt too young to know about fighter jets and satellites, subtly. But I kept this feeling a secret. He kept the voices in his head a secret from my sister and me. Once his father had been an alcoholic, but now his father was dead so that secret didn't mean much to anyone anymore. His mother was still alive, in her nineties. She had raised ten children: only one of them had committed suicide and only one of them had died by accidentally mixing chlorine with ammonia to scrub the kitchen floor. All the other brothers and sisters were alive and most of them worked at Caterpillar making earth-moving equipment. One of the brothers owned a roofing company and a Baskin Robbins. He used to give me ice cream coupons for my birthday which would infuriate my sister because he hadn't spent any real money. It was an old house and an old dining room table, since he and his wife, my mother, never threw anything out.

Poem

Let's not get carried away with meta-politeness. Literary theory is simply another kind of literature. It is as much philosophy as the warning on a package of nuts: *May Contain Nuts*. It is as much pornography as devouring a cashew the shape of a lover's dimple. It is as much eulogy as one can compose for a zit. Would that rhyme were so simple.

Against Elegy

Don't ask me to papier-mâché Jesus; I've tried. I wrote his obit years ago and every morning I look in the paper, but he's still not there. It's sad because I've not been paid for the writing yet. Maybe I'm overstating the case. Maybe the bird's eye view is too much about personal apocalypse. Apocalypse—the living burying the living in their best outfits. The question the poem attempts to answer is: Shall we really let the living plants in the living room die?

Good Mouth

At the end everyone seems, magically, to get his or her rank back in the world. The reasons for not sleeping with other men's wives have already been explained. Aristocratic households have servants, but servants have servants too. Loyalty through non-alliance or loyalty versus rivalry: Did you spend your wife's secrets at your best friend's house? Did you sacrifice your husband's virility for your mother's senility? Shakespeare, as usual, says it best: Excuse your sins more than your sins are. Part the pool by pissing in it, Cupid.

Self Portrait with Still Life

This portrait was repainted so many times that nobody is sure whether I was white or black underneath. San Francisco, again: The marketplace where they found my corpse wasn't very crowded. A few dawn-walkers, a stray mutt crapping on the leg of a lamppost, an earth-apple merchant setting up her stand. Under a still-lit lamplight, two teens haggled over a couple of pints of drug-free urine. There I was, lying on a bench in a crumpled-up, crapped-out position. My prick not yet hard, my words not yet purpled, my autopsy not yet a brief exam in failure. One-hundred and thirteen veins still ran through me. My mouth cracked open, toward its end, and all the world was at once scenery and seen. But I didn't much care. I wanted to sleep through the rest of the play none of us could play. One thousand times I set down my lines; one thousand times someone else picked them up.

About the Author

After receiving a BA in Political Science (Illinois Wesleyan University) including study in Vienna, Mark Yakich began graduate work in West European Studies, an interdisciplinary master's program, at Indiana University. There, he studied German and Dutch and wrote a master's thesis on European security and defense focusing on the ex-Yugoslavia. A research fellowship led him to Brussels, Belgium, where he stayed for two years working on an information and telecommunications project for the European Parliament. It seemed, for a time, that he had hit upon the ideal convergence of his training: politics, languages, and computers. It was, however, as a political consultant for the Parliament, that he began in depth to read American and world literature and to write. He soon realized that while the fields of politics and technology interested him, his passion was writing and studying literature. He redirected his energies and returned to the States to pursue an MFA in Creative Writing—first at Louisiana State University, then at the University of Memphis. He is currently completing a PhD in English (creative writing dissertation: a novel) at Florida State University, and is an Assistant Professor of English at Central Michigan University. Throughout his multifarious adventures in English at three graduate schools, including a two-year stint teaching at UC-Berkeley, he has worn many hats: poet, instructor, editor, radio show host, workshop leader, painter, photographer, and multimedia artist. In 2003, his first volume of poetry, *Unrelated Individuals Forming a Group Waiting to Cross,* was a winner of the National Poetry Series (selected by James Galvin) and was published by Penguin.